MY JOURNEY TO BECOMING A BETTER ME

BY: LANDRIS BARKER

Landris E. Barker Jr

Landris Barker is an Army Veteran with over 12 years of Fitness, Speaking and Coaching experience. Originally from Memphis, TN, Landris served 10 years in the US Army including a tour to Afghanistan in support of Operation Enduring Freedom (OEF) 2010-11. He has received many medals in the US Army to include the Army Achievement Medal and the Army Accommodation Medal. He holds a degree in communications and is currently pursuing a master's degree in Social Work. Landris plays piano and drums for his local church and is ordain clergy. He has a passion for helping others find themselves and facilitating them to their ultimate life goals. Barker is here to MOTIVATE, FACILITATE and produce RESULTS

Introduction

You are reading this because you feel there is more to you than who you right now. You don't feel you are at your highest potential. You know you can be better and could change your perspectives about things. Well…. you are reading the perfect book for this season in your life! This book will help guide, facilitate and motivate you on becoming a better version of yourself. I am extremely excited that you have made the first step, which is acknowledging that you are not where you want to be in life, and secondly, taking progressive action by reading this material. It may not seem like much now, but it is a big deal and very important, because without that acknowledgement, you will continue to allow your potential to go to waste, so let's get your journey started! I know you may be thinking, "how in the world is this guy going to help me, when he doesn't even know me?". You are correct about one thing, I do not know you or your situation (unless you are one of my clients, haha). I may not know that you feel stuck in a relationship with somebody you know you should not be with. I may not know that you are struggling to get through college for a degree that you really have no passion earning. I may not know that you are a single parent, trying to make ends meet for your kids. I may not know that your job is the most stressful thing in your life. I may not even know about that childhood trauma that still haunts you. One thing I do know however, is that you want better, and desire change in your life. No matter what situation you may be in, I have tools for you that will help you on this journey to becoming a better version of yourself. So, how does me not knowing your situation make me helpful? The answer is simple; it is because I will be speaking, guiding and motivating YOU! So regardless of the situation, you are the common denominator, and once we change your perspective, then everything around you will begin to shift. This is not a long drawn out book. Our attention span is not built that way, so I get straight to the point and dive into the "meat and potatoes". I want you to start experiencing change in the first few sentences of a chapter, not by the end or middle of the book. Who has time for that? So, with that being said, let's get started.

CHAPTER 1: GETTING TO KNOW YOURSELF

I know, I know.... You already know yourself, right? Who is better at knowing you, than you? I get it, and there is much truth to that. I also know that we can be pretty hard on ourselves. I have also discovered that we can be lenient on ourselves. It is not often that we have an unbiased opinion concerning ourselves. I challenge you to really dig deep, and look from within, and evaluate who you truly are. How do you do this? It's quite simple. You ask yourself "why" you do the things you do and have done. When you ask yourself "why", you get to the motive behind the action. Actions are results of emotions, values and motives. This will help you understand your own logic better. You will begin to see a perspective of you, that does beyond just the surface. Once we understand who we are, we have a true starting point on what needs to be changed in our lives. Trying to solve internal problems with surface solutions will only be temporary and ultimately have us back in a similar situation. Knowing who we truly are, also makes us better in relationships, because we can articulate this to those around us, so they can understand us as well. I'm sure you can think of one thing you do, just because you were raised that way, and not told the true meaning behind it. I remember growing up in church, and we would sing a "call and response" hymn. On the last stanza of that hymn, we would stand up until that stanza was finished and sit back down. I never knew why we did that, but it became second nature to me, and I thought it was abnormal when we went somewhere else that did not practice this. I later learned that this came from a practice in slavery times, when most African Americans could not read, to inform each other that the song was ending. After learning that, I never practiced it again because I knew better, and there was simply no need for that anymore. I don't want you living your life doing things that are keeping you from your goals, dreams and visions, because you failed to understand who you truly are, and never made the appropriate change. It's seems small and like it should not matter but it does. For example, it is a big difference between wanting a million dollars to help others and give back or wanting a million dollars to appear to be better than somebody else. So before moving on to the next chapters, really evaluate who you are so that you are making changes to your inner being and perspectives, and not just the surface of who you are.

Common Questions To Ask Yourself:

The following questions are general questions that can get you thinking about why you made certain choices in your life. These are not all the questions you should ask yourself, but they are questions that will help give you a better understanding of who you were, who you are, and who you want to be.

Why did I get married to my spouse?
Or
Why am I single?

Why did I go to college?
Or
Why didn't I go to college?

Why am I working at my current job or have my current career?
Or
Why am I unemployed at the moment?

What is the most important thing in my life right now? Why?

If I had 1 choice that I could change, what would that choice be? Why?

What is my biggest fear in life? Why?

Now you are really thinking about life. These simple inquiries of yourself has given you more perspective into your life. That is GREAT! Now let's dig a little deeper.

NOTES:

_____

_____

_____

_____

_____

_____

_____

_____

_____

_____

_____

_____

_____

CHAPTER 2: IDENTIFYING AND ELIMINATING INTERNAL BARRIERS

The first chapter was important because it made you evaluate from within and evaluate the "why" factor behind your choices. This practice help you identify the internal barriers in your life. Once you have assessed your motives, ask yourself, "is this productive or counterproductive to my dreams, goals and visions?". This question organizes your motives by productive motives or counterproductive motives. We must understand that counterproductive is not the same as "negative". We can be free of "negative" thoughts, emotions and values, and still have counterproductive motives. Here is an example: A business owner who does not like or have social media but, has products millennials would love to purchase. This business owner hates social media and refuses to get one because he does not want to see all the gossip and complaining people do on social media. This business owner's thoughts are not negative; however, they are counterproductive to him being successful at selling his products to millennials because 88% of millennials use social media according to manifest.com. His motives are understandable, he wants to stay away from negative vibes, but this thinking could potentially make him never reach his fullest potential. I want you to really identify and evaluate counterproductive thoughts, values, biased and emotions in your life, because these are barriers between who you are and who you want to be. Once you have identified these barriers, you simply begin to eliminate them. You do this by going against the grain. You may suddenly or gradually begin to do things opposite of your counterproductive bias, emotion, value and thoughts. I know it may appear as if you have to change your motives, but you don't. You just have to be strategic at how you carry out the action. This business owner can create business pages and advertise. He will avoid seeing timelines and stories, and still be able to sell effectively to millennials. He doesn't have to change his motive completely, but realize it is counterproductive to him succeeding, so eliminate the barrier and avoid what he doesn't want to see. This is a strategic compromise in accomplishing your goals dreams and visions.

Sometimes it is not as easy, and you will have to completely sacrifice things in your life in order to be successful and be a better version of yourself, but that is what this is all about; learning more about yourself and identifying ways to improve.

Something To Think About:

What is one goal you want to accomplish in the next 1-3 years?

What are your internal barriers? (Barriers you control)

Can you succeed with these counterproductive motives (strategic compromise)? If not, are you willing to change your motives completely?

Feel like you're interviewing yourself? Good! Interviews are designed in order to select the best candidate for a specific reason. You may not be the best candidate for your goals, dreams and visions right now. THAT IS A LIE! It's YOUR goal, your vision and your dream. Who better than YOU, and what better time than NOW? We just have to tweak a few things to make you successful, because it is a difference between being the best candidate and that candidate being successful. So, let's keep it moving to the next chapter. (This is going to be one of your favorites).

NOTES:

_____

_____

_____

_____

_____

_____

_____

_____

_____

_____

_____

CHAPTER 3: IDENTIFYING AND ELIMINATING EXTERNAL BARRIERS

You just identified internal barriers in your life. Emotions, values, thoughts and motives that stand between who you are and who you want to be. This can be very challenging because it is difficult to just change how we process things internally, or how we feel about a certain subject. Now you get the point the finger at something or someone else, haha. I had you identify and eliminate your own barriers first because, it prevents you from eliminating the wrong external barriers. Completing that first step, help you accurately identify external barriers. Many times, people get rid of individuals in their life thinking it will change the situation, but they find themselves in the same predicament. The only thing that change in their life was, now not having the support they once had. We point the finger and say, "if they wouldn't have", or "if that would have gone this way", yet we had internal barriers that became strongholds in our life. With self-evaluation, you can discern those counterproductive elements in your life. Again, it is a difference between negative, positive and productive and counterproductive. You could have positive people in your life, but they are counterproductive to you becoming a better version of yourself. I love examples so let's go with this; you have a friend who has positive vibes and will do almost anything for you. This friend is single, and you are married. This friend loves going out and attending parties. They always persuade you to go with them. You and your spouse are having problems, and you accuse trust issues in to why they don't want you going out. Your friend constantly tells you that you don't deserve that, and you should just leave. This cause you so much stress and now you are so focused on them, that you have no peace and you find yourself stuck. Many people will go about this wrong. They will eliminate the spouse for the friend. Some might even eliminate the friend for the spouse. In this situation, we know the friend is a counterproductive barrier. The strategic compromise here would be to simply say no to always going out with the friend yet keeping the friendship and always defending your vow to your spouse. It is challenging to take this action when you haven't gotten to know yourself and eliminated internal barriers. You will assess the situation accurately and make a choice that eliminates these external barriers, but not lose things important in your life. External elements do contribute to us becoming better versions of ourselves. You don't want to eliminate the wrong people from your life because you failed to evaluate situations inaccurately. Having that support system is important as you will learn in later chapters. Even though these barriers are external, guess who still has an impact on rather you succeed or not? You!

Let's Evaluate:

What are some external barriers in your life right now?

If it is a person, do you have to eliminate this person from your life? Or do you need to simply articulate to them that they are being counterproductive in your life?

What does life look like without this barrier? Will life be better, or will it be about the same?

What has prevented you from eliminating this barrier up to now?

Are you sure it is an external barrier or is it a barrier created by your own internal barriers?

Really think about these questions. They affect who and what remains in your life in order for you to become a better version of yourself. Being a better you is not really effective if you are not impacting anyone around you. It is hard to impact those around you if you have nobody around you to impact, right? Remember counterproductive and productive, not positive or negative. Let's keep reading, shall we?

NOTES:

_____

_____

_____

_____

_____

_____

_____

_____

_____

_____

_____

_____

CHAPTER 4: RE-EVALUATE WHO YOU ARE

I know, you just got to know yourself in chapter 1. Things have probably changed a little because you have removed internal and external barriers from your life (or so I hope). This can cause us to have a change in thoughts, valuesand motives. This chapter challenges you to assess if your goals, dreams and visions are the same. Re-evaluating who you are is very important and something you should do regularly. It is hard to articulate clearly to someone who you are, if you don't communicate with yourself concerning this matter. So, in chapter 1, you asked yourself "why" a lot. You must ask yourself the same question in this chapter. Maybe nothing changed about you but for some of you, I am sure it is not the same. Maybe you had an internal barrier and removed that from your thinking. You may have removed people from your life who contributed to your motives in chapter 1. An example of this would be, the reason behind wanting to accomplish a certain goal, because you wanted somebody to be proud of you, but that person was removed in chapter 3. Your "why' has changed, therefore you may even have the desire to accomplish this anymore. Assess life fromchapters 1-3 and evaluate if you lost anyone along the way. Did your desires change at all? Are your motives driven by the same internal elements as in chapter 1? This is important because, it's your journey and the goal is to be a better you. As your desires and passions change, you develop new internal and external barriers so you have to repeat chapter 2 and 3, and it is nothing wrong with that because you want to make sure you have peace and happiness with who you are becoming.

This chapter is simple, look at who you are, who you became between these chapters, and who you want to be. It is called self-maintenance. Like taking your car to get checked out or going to the doctor for a check-up. Nothing may have changed, but if so, let's engage it, re-focus and keep it moving. I already told you what to ask yourself for this chapter so refer to chapter 1's questions and meet me in chapter 4.

NOTES:

_____

_____

_____

_____

_____

_____

_____

_____

_____

_____

_____

_____

CHAPTER 5: KNOW YOUR PASSION/FUEL YOUR PASSION

So, you know yourself better than you ever have at this point (at least I hope you do). You have removed all these internal and external barriers between who you are now and who you want to be and want to accomplish. You have re- evaluated who you are right now currently. Now I want you to assess what you love. Doesn't have to be anything concerning your goals or who you aspire to be, but just something you love. Rather this is a hobby, person, event, location or anything. We all have a passion and most times, multiple passions. When you know what you are passionate about, you know what brings you peace, joy and happiness. The first few chapters should have extracted what your passion was. Now in this chapter, I want you to really know what your passion is, so that you can use this as a driving force to live out your fullest potential. The more you fuel your passion, the more peace you have. The more peace you have, the clearer you can think. The clearer you can think, the easier it is for you to create, develop and analyze. All of this makes you a powerful individual because there is literally nothing that can detour you from your pursuit. I have several passions. One passion of mine is helping others. No matter how angry, sad, frustrated or unmotivated I become, when I get the opportunity to help others, nothing else around me matters. I forget everything I am dealing with and lock in so that I can be of service to the person I am helping. This is easy for me because it is my passion and something I am motivated by and where I find peace. If you are not at peace right now in your life, you are most likely not fueling your passions. You are not doing whatever it is you love consistently. This can create a stressful, sad and uneventful pattern of life. You began to exist more than you are living. You have no desire for much and as a result you fall into a life slump. Please know or find your passion and begin fueling that passion to create peace around you so that you are in steady pursuit of your goals, visions and dreams.

Let's Evaluate:

What is/are your passion(s)?

How often are you practicing your passion(s)?

How does practicing your passion(s) make you feel?

What is preventing you from practicing your passion, if anything?

Really evaluate what drives you because it can be the difference between you succeeding or failing at whatever it is you may want to accomplish. So, you know what your passion is, so, DO IT!!! Do it often and consistently. You will see accelerated results. Let's move it right along shall we?

NOTES:

_____

_____

_____

_____

_____

_____

_____

_____

_____

_____

_____

_____

CHAPTER 6: GET FEEDBACK FROM OTHERS ABOUT HOW THEY VIEW YOU

So how do others view who you are? It doesn't matter what people think of you. BUT IT DOES in this case. How others view you and what they think of you is something you can't control. They have every right to have their own opinion about you. No matter what you do, somebody will have a negative connotation concerning you, and that is okay. So, what is the point then, right? The point of getting perspectives of others is to compare who they think you are, to who you truly are. This is beneficial because you can see areas of improvement and areas to sustain. Feedback from others provide you a 360-degree perspective of yourself. As stated before, you want to become a better version of yourself but how do you know you have truly succeeded? It is when your perspective of yourself matches the perspective of others. This does not mean you become who they want you to be. You may not meet the "requirements" or expectations others put on you, but you will have consistency in how others view you. It gives you affirmation that you have articulated to others who you truly are. No fronts or gimmicks but an authentic presentation of yourself. This practice could very well help change a counterproductive behavior, but ultimately you want to gain insight into what you are not articulating clearly. If others have a different perspective of you, it may be because you need to change behaviors, or you need to show them who you really are so their perspective of you changes. Do not use this practice to convince people of your "true colors". This practice is for you and not for them. They may never change their opinion of you, but it is pretty difficult to go against the truth, which is why it is important that you present an authentic you to others. Use this feedback as a tool to improvement. Don't get mad when you hear what others have to say. Again, it is THEIR perspective and opinion. Clearly, you have not articulated to them properly enough for them to see who you really are, or they still view you as the old you and that is ok, you just stay on track. Don't argue about it or tell anybody that they are wrong. I will give you a couple of questions to ask and it should help the conversation and intake go smooth.

So Let's Hear It:

Ask the following questions to somebody in the following areas of your life: Professional (work, career, business); Personal (family, friends, spouse/partner); Peers (distant acquaintances, church members, classmates)

What type of person do you view me as? What are your thoughts about me?

Why?

What do you think I could do better?

What do you think I could continue doing? What is something you enjoy about

me?

What is something you least enjoy about me?

These are basic questions that will give you a clear idea of how others view you. You can approach the person and just let them know that you are trying to get some honest assessments from them about you. Evaluate the answers people give you and take time to look within and reflect. Let's move right along.

NOTES:

_____

_____

_____

_____

_____

_____

_____

_____

_____

_____

_____

_____

CHAPTER 7: BREAK FREE FROM THE PAST

This is extremely difficult for some of us. Rather bad or good, sometimes it is hard to break free from our past. Most times, we associate the past as negatives things in our life, but I want you to break free from those accomplishments in your life that are keeping you from moving forward. What do you mean Landris? Well sometimes a past success can hinder us from future success. Think about sports teams who have won championships, who haven't even gone to a championship game since their last championship game. The Dallas Cowboys come to mind (sorry if that is your team, haha). Being successful before, doesn't guarantee success moving forward, so if you are still living off of yesterday's success, please evaluate your life and see if that is the very thing that is holding you back from moving forward and becoming a better version of yourself. It is difficult to see any improvements you need when you are living your life based off of a past success because you assume that method will always work and I am here to tell you, that is not how life works. We are constantly changing and things around us are steadily progressing. We must take on the attitude like Bill Bellichick, an NFL coach of the New England Patriots. He has been very successful, and he celebrates success, then he resets and figure out a way to be successful moving forward as if he never won anything. He is an "in the moment" type of planner. He looks at what is ahead and focus' on that. Now let's flip it around. We can't allow past failures and past events in our life to hinder us either. Before Bill Bellichick became successful, he was fired as the Cleveland Browns head coach. He didn't allow that experience to shape who he knew he could be. He believed in himself and moved forward. I know you have dealt with more than just being fired from a million-dollar job to get another million- dollar job, right? Many of you have experienced traumatic events in your life that makes you cry just thinking about them. Guess what? You are not what happened to you! Your future is promising and waiting on you to manifest it. Don't allow your pastto be a stronghold between you and peace. It is something that can't be changed, altered or erased. It happened and, no don't just "get over it", BUT DON'T let is keep you from all that potential success that is waiting for you. Let it go! Break free from it! You are about to excel, and you are going to need that peace within. Cry, scream and do whatever you have to do, but this is the last day for your past to keep you captive of becoming who you are destined to be.

NOTES:

_____

_____

_____

_____

_____

_____

_____

_____

_____

_____

_____

CHAPTER 8: BE GRATEFUL

So, we have broken free from everything in our past that was hindering us. In this chapter, we express gratitude. We deal with so many stressors in our life. We are busy people. Many have spouses, kids, jobs/careers, college, businesses, and so much more. This can make life pretty hectic. I know you want to complain about your boss and peers or your employees. Yes, your spouse frustrates you and the kids always keep your mind racing. With all that is going on and with all that has happened, I want you to take five minutes each day to reflect on things you are grateful for. It is hard to be mad, frustrated, depressed and anxious when you are being grateful. Expressing this gratitude not only drives the stress and negative thinking away, but it gives you hope and motivation to sustain those things in your life. Although it could be the job causing stress, be grateful for employment. Yes, those kids can be a handful, but I know you love them and are very grateful to have them in your life. Focus on why you are grateful for certain things in your life. I know your life can be a mess, but all of lives hit a storm at point or another. Yes, I know your problems are the worse in the world, but they really are not. There are people in worse scenarios than you right now. The fact that you are even reading this, is something to be grateful for. For starters, you had courage to make a change in your life. Secondly, you had enough money to purchase this book, or at least somebody who loves you to purchase it for you. Additionally, you have already made significant change in your life by completing all the chapters to this point. These are things to be grateful for. No matter how small or big, learn to be grateful because there are others who wish they had what you have, rather in tangible or intangible things. I know this is simple stuff, you already do this, but really reflect and lock in on the positive things in your life. Gratitude is important and brings out the joy we sometimes compress. You have more things than you know to be grateful for. The fact that you are not on fire right now, is a blessing. I know that is pretty dramatic, haha, but it's true. With gratitude comes appreciation, and appreciation makes you careful of how you handle whatever it is you are appreciative of. This ideology helps you to be diligent and not neglect those things in your life that bring you joy. Now let's express some gratitude and make it spread faster than a ….. I am not sure, but I wanted to use a southern phrase but could think of 1 so I will keep it moving, haha.

Think About It:

What are some things I am grateful for? Why? How would my life look without these things? What am I doing to keep these things in my life?

Yep, just three questions because it is cut and dry, straight to the point. When you identify what you grateful for and why you are grateful for them, you can express gratitude daily. You consistently work to sustain those things in your life and as a result, you are happier. Remember at least five minutes of gratitude, but feel free to express more. Feeling grateful? Good! Let's keep reading shallwe?

NOTES:

_____

_____

_____

_____

_____

_____

_____

_____

_____

_____

_____

_____

_____

CHAPTER 9: EVALUATE YOUR CIRCLE

Having a good support system is very important. I know you are independent and can do a lot on your own, but you must have the right circle and team around us to be successful. It is very important that the correct people are around you. Our circle can determine rather we succeed or fail. By now, you should have removed external barriers in your life. This was a big step but that is not the same as building a good support system. That step did allow you to remove toxic connections so at minimum right now, you are surrounded by decent connections. Now you must evaluate further to see who is apart of your support circle, and who are just mere acquaintances or casual connections. The example I used for external barriers was with the positive friend you had. They were positive but counterproductive. With the tools used in that chapter, you had an option to keep them around yet remove the barrier theypossessed. We evaluate in this chapter who is truly a supporter of our goals, dreams andvisions.

This is important because this friend is a true supporter of you, they just had counterproductive ways about them that were hindering your success. You identified and handled the situation accordingly, now they have become a true asset to you. I don't want you to lose true friends and genuine connections because you read the situation wrong. What does a true supporter look like? Someone who is honest with you, who pushes you towards success and not away from it, and one who you can be yourself around no matter what. If you can't express yourself freely without judgment, then re-evaluate their role in the circle. Now, disagreeing and judgment are different. They can disagree, give honest feedback and correct you without making you feel guilty about your expression, action or thoughts. As a life coach, I hear a lot that I don't agree with, but I never judge them and allow them to express themselves however they would like, but I do give an honest assessment without beating them up about it. Your circle is a reflection of who you are. You all may be different, but the common motive is quite the same, that is why you all connect in the first place. See why it is important to know yourself? You don't want to be supported by people you thought had the same common motives because you failed to know who you truly are. You can potentially fail at becoming the person you are destined to be. I will end the way I started the chapter, HAVING A GOOD SUPPORT SYSTEM IS VERY IMPORTANT. Evaluate your circle properly.

Let's Evaluate:

Who do I consider my support system right now?

Are they pushing me towards, or away from who I desire to be?

Can I express myself freely to these individuals? Do I trust the individuals in my

circle with my life?

Is there someone that I should consider to be apart of my circle that is not?
Why?

Do I need to remove people from my circle? Who? Why?

These questions will help with uncertainty in your support system. Please be diligent and take your time with this because it is delicate. So, I have some news for you. We are about to read the last chapter. Time flies when you're having fun. Last one to make it to the last chapter is a rotten egg. Yes, you are the rotten egg because I wrote the darn chapter, so of course I am there first, haha. And you are still reading this as if the last chapter is not ready to be read.

Still reading huh. Turn the darn page will you!

NOTES:

_____

_____

_____

_____

_____

_____

_____

_____

_____

_____

_____

_____

CHAPTER 10: THE JOURNEY DOESN'T END

I hate when good things end. Well, it doesn't have too! This book is only a quick guide. A good "pick me up" and motivation to get started and continue your journey to becoming a better you. I have given you the basic tools and resources to be successful. I expect to write many books in my lifetime that will help you in greater detail, but I needed to get the foundational framework to the world. Life gets deeper, more complicated and difficult but never neglect the basics. This journey you are on is for a lifetime. We are continually improving and pursuing better. Never stop growing. Never stop getting to know yourself. Do chapter 4 often because it could lead you to another chapter that you may have been neglecting in your life. I want you to understand that this is a cycle. The world is constantly changing, and we are constantly changing and there is nothing wrong with that, just ensure you can adapt when the change comes. I want you to know you are special. I want to encourage you to keep pressing, and you will be the person you were destined to be. This is only the beginning. You are the limit! There is life beyond the sky, so the sky is not the limit, you are. You are the limit because your potential is limitless! Keep that in mind. This is a journey and with any journey, you learn, see and experience so much. Yes, times will get hard and you will want to quit, BUT YOU BETTER KEEP GOING! If you don't have a life coach, get one! We are here to help and to make sure you live out your potential while providing that support to you. I recommend myself of course, haha. It does not matter who, but make sure they have your best interest in mind and not their own. IT'S YOUR JOURNEY, NOT THEIRS! It's all about YOU. I will leave my information. Let's connect and get you even further on this journey to becoming a better you.

What is something you learn about yourself that you didn't realize before?

Are you going to stay committed to becoming a better version of yourself?

Do you have a life coach? Are they meeting your needs as
a coach?

NOTES:

COMPARISON KILLS

When we realize there is need for change in our life, we should be looking at it from our own perspectives of where we are and where we inspire to be. Our dreams and goals should be based off our own desires and purpose. Many times, we pursue change in order to catch up to somebody else. We look at our life in comparison to theirs. This is very dangerous and can become a thief of manifestation in our life. We begin to change, and we ultimately see no results because we have skipped steps trying to reach a milestone that we are not prepared for. We must engage our purpose and our journey in the perspective of Time Zones. All across the world, there are different time zones. All time zones ultimately manifest but will always be on a different schedule. Germany will always see "tomorrow" before America. America is not behind its proposed schedule, just because Germany is already experiencing that particular day. We must understand, just because somebody else has reached a milestone in their life that you are inspiring to reach, doesn't mean that you are behind schedule. Don't allow these comparisons to rob you of your dreams, goals and success because you make un-necessary changes in your path or make the wrong type of changes. Be encouraged and stay the course. If you have not yet made a change, then let's start to this journey of transformation. Let's start this journey for YOU and not to reach the milestone of others.

Embrace Achievements

When ambitious people are pursuing goals and dreams, we tend to only look at what we have not accomplished, rather than what we have achieved. I want you to take a moment and reflect on the milestones that you have achieved so far. Some of us are between the age of 28-31, and just enrolled in college, yet we feel stagnate in life. In spite of the progressive action we have taken, we feel unaccomplished. Stop undervaluing your achievements and milestones. Even though you may not be where you want to be, you have achieved milestones in your life that others still inspire to achieve. Embrace your success and celebrate as if you already accomplished your overall goal, while still rigorously pursing your dreams. Continue to be GREAT!!

Set Milestones

In our life, we set goals and we have dreams we want to accomplish. We often time try to create a plan that only includes point "A" and point "B". We begin to get overwhelmed and frustrated, and slowly start to take detour from our goals or we drop them altogether. It's dangerous to take the "2 point" approach. We should set milestones for ourselves, so that we won't burn out. Milestones or checkpoints are great tools used to give yourself a consistent pace at achieving your goals. They give something to celebrate when you meet them, and they give you a moment to breathe before moving forward. Most of all sports are divided into halves or quarters in order to allow the players a chance to breathe and refocus on the goal. These milestones will also help you with any adjustments needed. Since you are not so burnt out, you can think clearly and ensure the plan you have is working or if you need to make necessary adjustments that are conducive to you achieving your goal. Make sure that your milestones align with your ultimate goal and dream, and not just a waste of your time because remember about "Eliminating Barriers". You don't want a milestone to become a hindrance to you, so set them carefully. You are fully capable of achieving your goals and dreams. Never give up and know that it is a marathon and not a sprint. Really think about what it takes to achieve the success you so desire. Ready, Set, GO!!!!!

Time Management

There are several things that keep us from achieving our goals. Of all the things that hinder us, TIME MANAGEMENT, is at the top of that list. We are sometimes good at setting goals; we have dreams and aspirations, but we simply never achieve anything because we waste too much time not acting. We complain consistently, play video and phone games, browse social media, watch TV and other things. We waste precious time, that could be invested in our goals, dreams and visions. We always say, "1 Day", but never declare that today is "Day 1" of me working towards my goals. Start doing fewer social media browsing, watching less TV, and fewer time complaining, and invest that time towards action! Start managing your time better and take advantage of those moments. You don't want to look back over your life and say, "I should have done more when I had the chance". I want you to know that you took advantage of every moment and opportunity presented to you!Time Management is extremely important and easier said than done, but that is why we have our Life Coaches, to help us prioritize and realize what is worth and not worth our time and energy.

Learning from Setbacks

Setbacks are often viewed as failures. Well that is FALSE! There will be times in your life where you try something, but it does not work out the way you anticipated, and you view it as failure. Scientist, manufacturers, engineers and others all have setbacks. These setbacks are not failures but lessons. They evaluate what they did and figure out why things did not go according to plan. We must do the same thing in our life. You DID NOT FAIL, you just need to evaluate what caused the setback. Once you have identified that, you try it again continue making in progress reviews and adjustments. Failure is not an option! Do not become stuck in life because you think you failed, this is only a setback and a life lesson that will help teach you so that you ultimately accomplish your goals.

THANK YOU SO MUCH

I just want to say thank you for reading my book. It really means a lot to me. I wrote this with your needs in mind. Again, I know I don't know you personally, but the type of person you are. You are clearly a "go getter" or you wouldn't have read or completed this book. I am very grateful that you allowed me to pour into you. I don't take this lightly. I wanted to write this book with a personal feel and not just a typical book barking orders or saying how amazing my program is for you. I wanted to connect with you and have you aware that I am a human like you, and I have most likely been where you are now. I make mistakes, and I am constantly learning as well. I am on my own journey of becoming a better me. Thank you for being a part of my journey. Thanks to God almighty, Jesus Christ my Savior, for without Him nothing is possible by which I do. Thanks to my beautiful wife Jocelyn for her support and love. My kids, Joseph, Isaiah, Landon, Emmanuel and Zoey, I love you. Thanks to my parents Landris Sr and Shirley for being great. To my grandma Veria who raised me for the most part with my parents. Thanks to all who support me, my friends and family, I love you all! Thanks to my clients for untrusting me with delicate situations in your life, without you all I am not who I am as a life coach. Thanks to the publishing company, editors, just EVERYBODY! THANK YOU, THANK YOU, THANK YOU!

-Coach Landris

Landris Barker

Certified Life Coach www.coachlandris.org

Contact Coach Landris info@coachlandris.org

**youtube.com/coachlandris facebook.com/coachlandris
intragram.com/landrisbarker**

NOTES:

NOTES:

NOTES:

NOTES:

NOTES:

_____

_____

_____

_____

_____

_____

_____

_____

_____

_____

_____

_____

_____

NOTES:

_____

_____

_____

_____

_____

_____

_____

_____

_____

_____

_____

_____

NOTES:

NOTES:

NOTES:

_____

_____

_____

_____

_____

_____

_____

_____

_____

_____

_____

_____

NOTES:

_____

_____

_____

_____

_____

_____

_____

_____

_____

_____

_____

_____

CPSIA information can be obtained
at www.ICGtesting.com
Printed in the USA
LVHW011133170820
663373LV00003B/292